FOR THE BIRDS:
WOMEN COMPOSERS

MUSIC HISTORY SPELLER
VOLUME 1, SECOND EDITION

I0167368

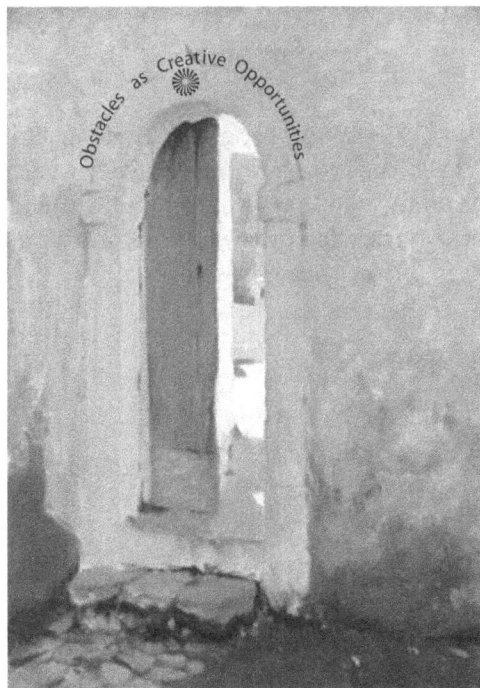

Obstacles as Creative Opportunities

MIRIAM ZACH

Culicidae
PRESS, LLC
culicidaepress.com

Ames | Gainesville | Lemgo | Rome
2015

Culicidae Press
918 5th Street
Ames, IA 50010
www.culicidaepress.com

Second Edition

ISBN-13:   978-1-941892-10-7
ISBN-10:   1941892108

Graphic design and layout by polytekton.com © 2015
Image on page 1 entitled *Open Doorway, Morocco*, by John Singer Sargent (1856-1925). Image from http://www.jssgallery.org/Paintings/10057.htm, accessed August 19, 2005; image modified by misumi-waDesign

1. Music 2. Music Theory 3. Music History 4. Music Pedagogy   I. Miriam Zach

To Margaret, Herbert, Mikesch, friendly four-footed feline Sara,
and all the birds who are free to fly

TABLE OF CONTENTS

INTRODUCTION

Welcome to an international archeology-of-knowledge journey beginning more than 4000 years ago. We will explore relatively unknown intellectual territory traversing the world, using an international code to decipher the meaning hidden in musical symbols, and examine intellectual artifacts in the history of ideas that we discover along the path.

To begin the search I consulted the following reference works for information on women composers' lives and works. I hope it is your quest to continue to investigate and to create.

Miriam S. Zach,
Gainesville, July 2015

BIBLIOGRAPHY

Cohen, Aaron I. *International Encyclopedia of Women Composers.* 2nd edition. (2 volumes) New York: Books & Music (USA) Inc., 1987.

Olivier, Antje & Sevgi Braun. *Komponistinnen aus 800 Jahren.* Essen: Sequentia Verlag, 1996.

Sadie, Julie Anne & Rhian Samuel, editors. *The Norton/Grove Dictionary of Women Composers.* New York: W.W. Norton & Company, 1995.

DISCOGRAPHY

Zach, Miriam. *Hidden Treasures: 300 Years of Organ Music by Women Composers.* Recorded in Princeton University Chapel, 1998.

For on-line resources including an expanded bibliography and links to sheet music/CDs please go to http://www.womencomposerslibrary.org

HOW TO USE THIS BOOK

In a series of 25 biographies that combine words and music notes, this book will teach you how to read music at the same time that you learn about the amazing lives of past and current women composers.

There are multiple ways in which you can use this book:
   • First you can read the stories, replacing each written music note with the correct letter as you read it.
   • Secondly, you can write the corresponding letter of each music note underneath each staff in the stories to complete the music-encoded sentences.
   • Thirdly, once you have figured out the names of the notes, you can play them on the instrument of your choice.

The book is graded, i.e. the notes become increasingly more difficult to read as the range and the clefs vary. The first four biographies use only the treble clef; the next four stories use only the bass clef; finally, the last seventeen biographies combine alternating treble and bass clefs.

This is the first volume in a series of books about the life and work of women composers. Keep checking our website at http://www.womencomposerslibrary.org for future books and other related information.

Treble Clef

B C D E F G A B C

G A B C D E F G A

Bass Clef

D E F G A B C D E

B C D E F G A B C

Here are some mnemonic devices to help you remember the names of the notes. The notes *between* the staff lines for the treble clef spell the word **F**-**A**-**C**-**E**, and the notes *on* the lines spell **E**very **G**ood **B**ird **D**oes **F**ine.

F A C E   E G B D F

For the bass clef the notes *between* the staff lines spell **A**ll **C**ows **E**at **G**rass, and the notes *on* the lines spell **G**ood **B**irds **D**o **F**ine **A**lways.

A C E G   G B D F A

Also please note that ♯ means 'sharp', ♭ means 'flat', and ♮ means 'natural'. Enjoy!

ENHEDUANNA (C. 2285-2250 B.C.E.)

Image from http://www.geocities.com/fegarc/Enheduana.html, accessed July 30, 2005; image modified by misumiwaDesign

Enh - uanna is - l - rat - as pro - ly th - rliest known nam - omposer an - uthor. She wrote in cuneiform more than 4300 y - rs - o. Anonymous scri - s wrot - ore her, but she i - ntifi - herself in first person in her writings, and thus her name was not . She was a Sumerian high priestess of the Moongod Nann - t Ur (ancient Iraq). She was th - ughter of King Sargon of Akk -, who was th - irst ruler of Sumeria to unite northern

8

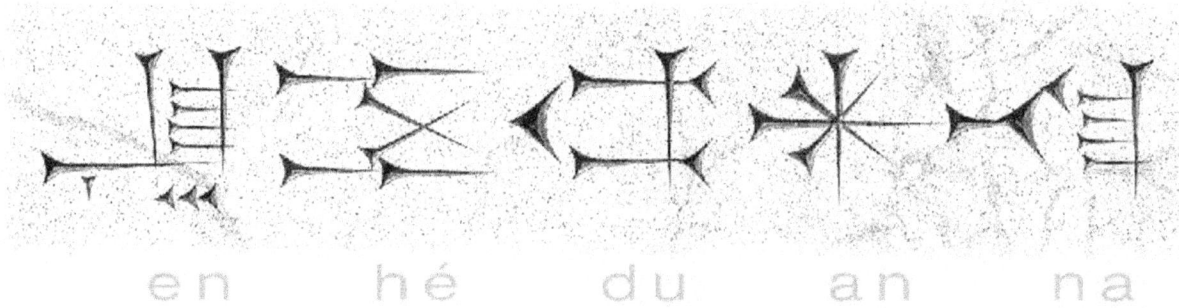

and southern Mesopotamia. Her mother was Sumerian from southern Mesopotamia.

Enh - [musical notation] - uanna's name m - [musical notation] - ns "The High Priestess [nam - [musical notation]]

Ornament of the Sky" (*en*=High Priestess, *h* - [musical notation] - *u*=Ornament, *Ana*=of the

Sky/H - [musical notation] - ven). She is cr - [musical notation] - it - [musical notation] for having written a hymn cycle

of in - [musical notation] - ntations/songs to Inanna, the go - [musical notation] - ss of

Lov - [musical notation] - nd War, as well as *The Sumerian Temple Hymns*, 42 hymns to the temples

of Sumer an - [musical notation] - kk - [musical notation] .

KASSIA (B. 810)

Image from http://www.chass.utoronto.ca/~chatzis/Troparion.htm, accessed July 30, 2005, modified by misumiwaDesign

Kassia was an important Gr- -k composer of M- -ieval Byzantin- -hant, and author of s- -ular poetry. She is i- -ntifi- by di- -rent names, Kasian- , -si- , -n- -ikasia. She was consider- to the most -utiful and intelli- -nt bri- -l -ndi- -te for Emperor Theophilos (829-842). -ording to M- -ieval l- -nd, when the Emperor was

10

-out to give Kassia th- -pple indi- -ting he

-vor- her to his bride, he

-moan- that evil ha- -ome to the world through

women. Kassi- -nswer- that women also

h- -rought much good, in reference to the birth o- -hrist.

Ther- -ter, Kassia -m- nun in

-onvent where she compos- numerous

s- -r- melodies for religious -stivals, and

s- -ular poems.

HILDEGARD VON BINGEN (1098-1179)

German postal stamp in honor of Hildegard von Bingen's 900-year anniversary, modified by misumiwaDesign

Hil - rd von Bingen was - mous - rman composer, author and mystic - tive in the M - ieval era, whose 900th birthy - r was - l - rat - in 1998.

From an aristocrati - mily, she was - pt - into a p - ul - n - ictin - y and later - m - ss at Ruperts - rg in the Rhine valley n - r the vill - of Bin - n. Hil - rd is known for her coll - tion of s - r - lyri - l poetry in Latin with cr - tive im - ry and melodies written in - rly neume notation (*Symphonia armonie - lestium revelationum*), and

M - [music] - ieval chants in a s - [music] - r - [music] morality play (*Ordo virtutum*)

presenting a mysti - [music] - l [music] - ttl - [music] - tw - [music] - n

the [music] - vil and sixt - [music] - n Virtues for the soul, Anima. In

[music] - ition, Hil - [music] - rd wrote [music] - out the prophetic visions

she experien - [music] (*Scivias*), [music] history and m - [music] - ical

tr - [music] - tises (*Physi* - [music] and [music] - *use et cure*), and

correspon - [music] with religious and politi - [music] - l l - [music] - rs.

Her spirit [music] - i - [music] - s in the h - [music] - rts and minds of international

scholars who continue to r - [music] -, translate, perform, r - [music] - ord, and

writ - [music] - out her li - [music] - and i - [music] - s in a myri - [music]

of langu - [music] - s.

Maddalena Casulana (c. 1540- c. 1583)

M - 🎵 - len - 🎵 - sulana was an Italian singer, lutenist, and Renaiss - 🎵 - omposer of th - 🎵 - irst known m - 🎵 - ri - 🎵 - ls by a woman to publish - 🎵. In thr - 🎵 - ooks of m - 🎵 - ri - 🎵 - ls print - 🎵 in 1568, 1570, and 1583, she set her own poetry and that o - 🎵 - ontemporaries to music, intri - 🎵 - tely interw - 🎵 - vin - 🎵 - our an - 🎵 - ive voi - 🎵 - s in 🎵 - ontrapuntal textur - 🎵 - nd using word painting popular in her time. Sh - 🎵 - i - 🎵 - t - 🎵 *Il Primo Libro di*

Image from http://www.lamediatheque.be/travers_sons/fc-casulana.htm, accessed July 30, 2005, modified by misumiwaDesign

M - ri - li a quattro voci (Veni- , 1568) to

Is - ll - M - ici Orsina, an aristocratic

musi - l patron. M - lena's compositions also

app - r - in coll - tions of musi - y

various - mous musicians, Il - si - rio,

Book I (1566). International authors have written - out her i - s

in a variety of langu - s includin - nglish, French, - rman,

and Italian.

FRANCESCA CACCINI (1587-1645)

Image from http://en.wikipedia.org/wiki/Francesca_ Caccini. accessed July 30, 2005, modified by misumiwaDesign

Fran - ♪ -s- ♪ ♪ - ini

was an Italian singer, harpsichordist

and prolifi - ♪ ♪ - omposer from

Floren - ♪ who work - ♪ in the

M - ♪ - ici court. She was th - ♪ - irst woman known to compose operas,

♪ La li - ♪ - razione di Ru - ♪ - iero ♪ - ll'isola d'Alcina

(1625). From a musi - ♪ - l ♪ - mily, Fran - ♪ - s - ♪ was

the ♪ - ughter o - ♪ - omposer Giulio ♪ - ini, who was a

mem - ♪ - r of th - ♪ - lorentin - ♪ - merata, and

one of the cr - ♪ - tors of th - ♪ - xpressive 'new music' of the

- roqu - ♪ - ra that ♪ - n ♪ - out 1600.

Their new style of *monody*, or solo song with instrumental ♩ - ompaniment,

and their *stile rappresentativo*, ♩ - ramatic r - ♩ - itative style in which

melodies mov - ♩ - fr - ♩ - ly over ♩ - oun - ♩ - tion

of simpl - ♩ - hords, 1 - ♩ - to the invention of opera.

Fran - ♩ - s - ♩ - 's *Il Primo Libro* ♩ - *lle musiche* (1618) is one of the

lar - ♩ - st coll - ♩ - tions of ♩ - rly ♩ - roque

s - ♩ - red and s - ♩ - ular monody. Her

remark - ♩ - 1 - ♩ - ilities and musi - ♩ - 1 contributions

continue to ♩ - 1 - ♩ - rat - ♩ - in con - ♩ - rts and

publi - ♩ - tions to - ♩ - y.

ELIZABETH CLAUDE JACQUET DE LA GUERRE (1665-1729)

Le Parnasse francois (1732) by Titon du Tillet; image from http://
www.ambache.co.uk/wGuerre.htm, accessed July 29, 2005,
modified by misumiwaDesign

Eliza- ♪ -th Clau- ♪ Jacquet ♪ la Guerre was a ♪ -l- ♪ -rat- ♪ French composer, virtuoso harpsichordist and or- ♪ -nist who was ♪ -tive in the ♪ -roque era. She ♪ -m- ♪ -rom a musi- ♪ -l- ♪ -mily in Paris, was ♪ -ughter of or- ♪ -n buil- ♪ -r Clau- ♪ J- ♪ -quet, and wife of or- ♪ -nist Marin ♪ la Guerre. -ore the ♪ -rly ♪ of ten, she ♪ -rned public -laim for her ex- ♪ -ptional natural aptitu- ♪ -ing -le to sightr- ♪ , sin- ♪ , ♪ -ompany herself and others on the harpsichord, and improvise pi- ...... -s. ...... -r to

h- ...... -r and encour- ...... this "wonder child," King Louis XIV

invit- ...... Eliz- ...... -th to ...... musician in his court. She

wrote and publish- ...... harpsichord compositions (*Pi-* ...... *-s* ......

-lav- ...... *-in*, 1687), an oper- ...... *-phale et Procris* (1694),

cham- ...... -r music (...... four *Trio Sonatas* for two violins, viol- ......

...... -m- ...... , and or- ...... -n (1695), six violin sonatas (1707)), and

twelve s- ...... -r- .... -ntatas ...... -s- ...... on Old Testament

stories (1708, 1711). Soon ...... -ter her ...... -th an engrav- ......

m- ...... -llion with her nam- ...... im- ...... was

cr- ...... -t- ...... to commemorate her li- ...... and work.

ANNA AMALIA, DUCHESS OF SAXE-WEIMAR (1739-1807)

Image from http://www.answers.com/topic/anna-amalia-duchess-of-saxe-weimar-eisenach, accessed July 30, 2005, modified by misumiwaDesign

Ann - 𝄢 𝄢 - mali - 𝄢 ,

𝄢 - uchess of Saxe - Weimar, was

a 𝄢 - rman Classi - 𝄢 - l

composer of instrumental and vo - 𝄢 - l

music, pianist, and patron, who

𝄢 - lon - 𝄢 to a

musi - 𝄢 - l 𝄢 - mily. She was a ni - 𝄢 of

Kin - 𝄢 𝄢 - r - 𝄢 - rick th - 𝄢 𝄢 - r - 𝄢 - t of Prussia

who rul - 𝄢 𝄢 - t th - 𝄢 - ourt of Sans Souci and play - 𝄢

th - 𝄢 𝄢 - lute. His two sisters also compos - 𝄢 music, namely Wilhelmine

von 𝄢 - yreuth (1709 - 1758), an - 𝄢 𝄢 - nn - 𝄢 𝄢 - malia,

20

Prin - [music notation] -ss of Prussia (1723 - 1787) who was [music notation] - mous for

est - [music notation] - lishin - [music notation] music library (*Amalienbibliothek*) in [music notation] - rlin.

Ann - [music notation] - malia's *Singspiel* [opera] named *Erwin un* - [music notation] - *lmire* (1776)

on a text by Johann Wol - [music notation] - ng von Goeth - [music notation] - monstrates her

knowl - [music notation] o - [music notation] - ontemporary Italian opera. In the town of

Weimar she pro - [music notation] to encour - [music notation] intell - [music notation] - tual

li - [music notation] - y bi - [music notation] - in - [music notation] - uthors, [music notation]

J. W. von Goeth - [music notation] - nd J. G. Her - [music notation] - r, an - [music notation] - omposers

to [music notation] - ther in a "court of the muses." Her consi - [music notation] - r - [music notation] - l - [music notation]

- oll - [music notation] - tion o - [music notation] - ooks is in the *Zentralbibliothek*

[music notation] - r [music notation] - *utschen Klassik* in Weimar.

MARIA THERESIA VON PARADIS (1759-1824)

Image from http://www.mark-hammond.co.uk/edmusic2.htm, accessed July 30, 2005, modified by misumiwaDesign

Maria Theresia von Par - is

was an Austrian composer,

t - her, and pianist from

Vienna, who - m -

- lin - - t the

of thr - .

She h - ulous memory for music, and

- velop - - r - r composing and

performing piano con - rts in Austri - , - nglan - ,

- ran - , - rmany, and Switzerlan - - urin -

- s - ter her eyesight h - . Maria

visit - Wol - n - m - us Mozart in Salzburg who - i - t - piano con - rto to her, and - rl Philipp Emanuel - h in Hamburg. She compos - piano pi - s, songs, and operas in the Classi - l period, with th - ssistan - of a note typesetting m - hine, invent - for her by Johann Ri - inger. Maria help - Valentin Haüy cr - te th - irst school for th - lind in Paris in 1785. She est - lish - her own music school for - males in 1808 in Vienna where she taught piano, voi - , and music theory.

Maria Agata Szymanowska (1789-1831)

Mari - [music] - ta Szymanowska was a Polish con - [music] - rt pianist in th - [music] - ourt of the Russian Tsar in St. Petersbur - [music] - nd Romanti - [music] - omposer. She wrote more than one hundr - [music] - songs and piano pi - [music] - s, many - s - [music] on folk melodies, and Polish - [music] - n - [music] - s, the polonais - [music] - nd mazurka. Maria, who studi - [music] with th - [music] - nglish composer John Field, is also known for her nocturnes. She dissolv - [music] - her marri - [music] - with a w - [music] - lthy Polish landowner, and pro - [music] - to perform con - [music] - rt en- ments on st- s in -lgium, England,

Fran- , -rmany, Holland, Polan- , -nd Russia. Maria

inspir- the -m- author Johann

Wol- -ng von Goethe to writ- poem, *Aussöhnung*

(R- -onciliation). Among those who visit- Maria in St. Petersburg

were -mous composers of her time including Ludwig van

-thoven, Fr- -ri- -hopin, Franz Liszt,

Robert an- -lara Schumann, an- -io- -hino

Rossini.

CLARA WIECK SCHUMANN (1819-1896)

Clara Schumann on German 100 DM bill (no longer in circulation); image from http://www.schumann.jp/clara/clara02.html, modified by misumiwaDesign

Clara Wi - ♪ - k Schumann was ♪ - rman Romanti - ♪ - omposer and virtuoso pianist ♪ - mous for her expert t - ♪ - hnique, ♪ - utiful tone, and ♪ - pth of ♪ - ling. She was ♪ - hild prodigy and ♪ - ughter of pro - ♪ - ssional musicians. In 1840 she marri - ♪ - omposer Ro - ♪ - rt Schumann with whom she ha - ♪ - ight children. In spite of di - ♪ - icult challen - ♪ - s ♪ - lancing her ♪ - r - ♪ - r, ♪ - mily responsibilities, her hus - ♪ - nd's illness, and the prevalent contemporary attitu - ♪ - that doubt - ♪ - women's cr - ♪ - tiv - ♪ - ility, Clar - ♪ - omposed numerous piano pi - ♪ - s (♪ *Scherzo* op. 10), songs, orchestral (♪ *Piano*

Con - ♪ - *rto* op. 7) an - ♪ - ham - ♪ - r works (♪ *Piano Trio* op. 17).

She also taught piano, and ♪ - ve con - ♪ - rts. ♪ - ter Ro - ♪ - rt's

♪ - th in 1856, Clar - ♪ - ontinu - ♪ her international performing

♪ - r - ♪ - r tourin - ♪ - ontinental Europ - ♪ - n - ♪

♪ - ngland. She play - ♪ her own compositions and piano solos by her hus - ♪ - nd,

J.S. ♪ - h, ♪ - thoven, Chopin, Liszt, ♪ - lix Men - ♪ - lssohn,

and her li - ♪ - lon - ♪ - riend Johannes Brahms. In 1878 sh - ♪ - me

♪ - ir - ♪ - tor o - ♪ piano master class at the *Hoch'sche Konservatorium* in Frankfurt.

Her ex - ♪ - ptional cr - ♪ - tive talent is r - ♪ - ogniz - ♪

to - ♪ - y in many r - ♪ - ordings and publi - ♪ - tions in di - ♪ - rent

langu - ♪ - s.

LILI'OUKALANI, QUEEN OF HAWAII (1838-1917)

Image from Hawaii State Archives showing Queen Lilioukalani of Hawaii; modified by misumiwaDesign

Lili'oukalani, Qu- [♪] -n of Hawaii compos- [♪] many songs, some under the pseudonym Mme. Aorena. Her

He mele lahui Hawai'i (Honolulu, 1867) [♪] -me the Hawaiian national anthem, and her son- [♪] -*loha 'oe* ([♪] -rewell to th- [♪]) (San Francisco, 1878) has [♪] -quir- [♪] international [♪] -me. Lon- [♪] -ore the islands [♪] -me part of th- [♪] -ifty Unit- [♪]

States in 1959, Qu- [♪] -n Lili'oukalani m- [♪] an [♪] -ort to synthesize Hawaiian and western Europ- [♪] -n music. From a musi - -l - mily, she play - the piano, or - n,

and was an - pt sight r - r of Western musi - -l

notation. She studi - music with Henry - r - r,

- rman military - ndl - r who was sent

to Hawaii by the *Kaiser* at Kamehameha V's request. Qu - n Lili'oukalani

reign - - rom 1891 until 1893 when she was - pos -

by Ameri - - ns who were interest - in Hawaii's su - r

and pin - - ppl - - rops. Her book, *Hawaii's Story by Hawaii's*

Qu - n (Boston, 1898), a coll - - tion of manuscripts, letters, and

print - musi - - n - ound in the Hawaii

Stat - - rchives in Honolulu.

AGATHE URSULA BACKER-GRØNDAHL (1844-1907)

- the Ursul - ker Grøn - hl was a prolific Norw - ian Romanti - omposer and internationally distinguish - on - rt pianist from Christiania (now Oslo), who was ontemporary o - var - ri - . She studi - piano at the Theodor Kullak my in rlin, then with Hans von Bülow in Floren - , nd ranz Liszt in Weimar. Sh - ve piano con - rts in Norway, Sw - n, Finlan - , rmany, Englan - , n - ran - , includin - performan - o - ri - 's *Piano Con* - rto at the Paris Exhibition of 1889. Although sh - 🎵 - r - 🎵 - ually 🎵 - me h - 🎵 - ring impair - 🎵 ,

🎵 - the wrote many compositions including piano pi - 🎵 - s (

Seren - 🎵 op. 15 (1882), 🎵 - ll - 🎵 op. 36 (1895),

I bl - 🎵 - jellet (On th - 🎵 - lue Mountain) suite op. 44 (1897), her

techni - 🎵 - lly challenging Con - 🎵 - rt Etu - 🎵 - s), and

arran - 🎵 - ments of Norw - 🎵 - ian folk songs an - 🎵 - nces. She

also wrote numerous songs (🎵 Th - 🎵 - hild's Sprin - 🎵 - y op.42

(1899), and a son - 🎵 - ycle on poems by A. Jyn - 🎵). Her sister Harriet 🎵

- ker (1845 - 1932), a well-known painter of interiors who travell - 🎵 - xtensively with

🎵 - the in Europ - 🎵 , 🎵 - st - 🎵 - lish - 🎵 - n art school in Oslo

which 🎵 - velop - 🎵 into the National Art 🎵 - my.

CHIQUINHA GONZAGA (1847-1935)

Image from http://www.antjeschrupp.de/chiquinha_gonzaga.htm, accessed August 8, 2005; image modified by misumiwaDesign

Chiquinha (Francis - ♪ H - ♪ - wi - ♪ - s Neves) Gonz - ♪ was a popular and prolifi - ♪ - razilian composer, pianist, social ♪ - tivist, an - ♪ - onductor from Rio de Janeiro who was du - ♪ "th - ♪ - minine O - ♪ - n - ♪ - h." In 1885 she was th - ♪ - irst woman to conduct an orchestra in Brazil. She was ener - ♪ - tic in the movement to fr - ♪ slaves in her homeland, and th - ♪ - laration of the Republic. Chiquinh - ♪ - ompos - ♪ orchestral, ♪ - n - ♪ - ham - ♪ - r, piano, vo - ♪ - l and

32

th - ♪ - tre music. Many of her ♪ - n - ♪ - s were

publish - ♪ including h - ♪ - neras, polkas, tangos (♪ her

- mous O ♪ - *úcho* (1895)), marches (♪ O ♪ - *realas*

(1899) for ♪ - rnival), mazurkas, and waltzes. ♪ - tw - ♪ - n

1885 and 1933 she wrote scores for operettas includin - ♪ - *orrobodó* (1912) which

h - ♪ more than 1500 performan - ♪ - s, and *Maria* (1933), and 77 plays.

From 1902 until 1910 she travel - ♪ in Englan - ♪ - ran - ♪,

Italy, Portu - ♪ - l, and Spain, then return - ♪ to Rio ♪ Janeiro,

where she ♪ - m - ♪ - ounding mem - ♪ - r of the

Soci - ♪ - *razileir* - ♪ - *utores T* - ♪ - *trais.*

TERESA CARREÑO (1853-1917)

Image from http://w1.neuronnexion.fr/~goninet/carreno.htm, accessed August 8, 2005; image modified by misumiwaDesign

Teres - ♪ - rreño

was a Venezuelan virtuoso pianist, opera

sin - ♪ - r, conductor, and

Romanti - ♪ - omposer of primarily

piano pi - ♪ - s with

t - ♪ - hni - ♪ - lly

di - ♪ - icult pass - ♪ - s of octaves, trills, and l - ♪ - ps. Her

style is ♪ - lend of South and North Ameri - ♪ - n folk melodies,

an - ♪ - urop - ♪ - n - ♪ - n - ♪ - s,

esp - ♪ - ially the waltz. She was th - ♪ - ran - ♪ - ughter

o - ♪ - omposer Jos - ♪ - rreño, grandni - ♪ - of Simon

Bolivar, to whom sh- -i- -t- hymn, and piano

student of Ameri- -n composer Louis Gottschalk. In 1862, her -mily

emigrat- to New York -use of civil uph- -val in

Venezuel- . At the of ten, she tour- the

Unit- States playing for -raham Lincoln at the White House. In 1866

Teresa travel- to Europe wher- -io- -hino Rossini

an- -ranz Liszt were in- impress- by her

talent. She also tour- S- -ndinavi- -n-

-ustrali- -s -on- -rt pianist.

-ter her -th, the Teres- -rreño Museum was

est- -lish- in her honor in -r- -s, Venezuela.

DAME ETHEL SMYTH (1858-1944)

Dame Smyth is an internationally [♪] - laim - [♪] - nglish author and composer of operas ([♪] *The Wreckers* [♪] - out the s - [♪]), Romantic *Li* - [♪] -*r*, orchestral pi - [♪] - s, and cham - [♪] - r music. At 19 y - [♪] - rs of [♪] , she l - [♪] - t London with her [♪] to study at the Leipzig Conservatory. In Germany, Ethel met Johannes Brahms, [♪] - var - [♪] - ri - [♪] , [♪] - lara Schumann, and Peter Tchaikovsky who [♪] - me gr - [♪] - t composers. Despite opposition from her parents and publishers, Ethel [♪] - i - [♪] not to [♪] - or discour - [♪] , but to go ah - [♪] st - [♪] - ily [♪] - veloping [♪] - r - [♪] - r as a composer. She

36

- m - l- - r in the women's su - - r -

movement and wrote her - mous *March of the Women* (1911) which was th -

- nthem sun- - t m - - tings - vo - - tin -

- qual rights for -males. Also, she - n

- r - - r as an author, su - - ing to write ten books,

- use performances of her music on th- - ontinent

wer - - nn - - uring World War I, and she was - oming

. Ethel Smyth r - - iv - many

- ol - - s, an honorary Doctor of Music at Oxford University

in 1926, for her - l - - ti - - ility to - sorb

i - - s, and - s of pion - - ring - orts.

AMY MARCY CHENEY BEACH (1867-1944)

Image from http://www.seacoastsearch.com/ nhlinks/people/amybeach/, accessed August 9, 2005; image modified by misumiwaDesign

Amy Marcy Cheney ♪ - h is an Ameri - ♪ - n virtuoso pianist and prolific composer from New England. She cr - ♪ - t - ♪ - out 300 Romantic art songs, s - ♪ - ular and s - ♪ - r - ♪ - horal works (♪ *Mass in E Major*, 1890), orchestral (♪ her ♪ - l - ♪ - rat - ♪ lar - ♪ - s - ♪ - l - ♪ - lic *Symphony in e-minor*, 1896), piano pi - ♪ - s (♪ *Hermit Thrush*), and cham - ♪ - r works. She was ♪ - hild prodigy with ♪ - ulous memory, per - ♪ - t pitch, an - ♪ - ility to conn - ♪ - t keys with colors. Her family, ♪ - rly in her li - ♪ , ♪ - ncour - ♪ her ♪ - p - ♪ - ilities. Her mother, a talent - - mateur musician, gl - - ly agr -

to her first piano t - - her, an - - my taught herself

counterpoint and orchestration. At th - of 16, Amy m - her

- ut as pianist in Boston. - ter marrying Dr. H. H. - h in

1885,   she - i - to focus on composition until his

- th in 1911. Then Mrs. - h pro - to perform

her own music in Europe, which incr - - s - her - me.

- ginning in 1921 she was - llow at the M - - owell

Colony, and in the y - - r 1925 she help - - r - - te the

Society of Ameri - - n Women Composers.

NADIA BOULANGER (1887-1979)

Image from http://www.classicalcompos ers.org/cgi-bin/ccd.cgi?comp=boulanger_ nadia, accessed August 9, 2005; image modified by misumiwaDesign

N - ♪ - i - ♪ - oulan - ♪ - r was ♪ - rench composer, or - ♪ - nist, conductor, an - ♪ - mous composition t - ♪ - her from a musi - ♪ - l - ♪ - mily. Her ♪ - ther an - ♪ - ran - ♪ - ther both taught musi - ♪ - t the Paris Conservatoire, and her mother was a sin - ♪ - r. At the Conservatoire N - ♪ - ia studi - ♪ - or - ♪ - n with Louis Viern - ♪ - n - ♪ - lexan - ♪ - r Guilmant, an - ♪ - omposition with ♪ - riel ♪ - ur - ♪ - n - ♪ - harles Marie Widor. In 1908 she won s - ♪ - ond pl - ♪ for the Rome Prize for her ♪ - ntata *La Sirene*. Sh - ♪ - ompos - ♪ - other vo - ♪ - l (*Les heures claires* (1910) with Raoul Pugno) and instrumental works. ♪ - ter th - ♪ - rly

40

-th of her youn- ♪ -r sister, ♪ -m- ♪ -omposer Lili Boulan- ♪ -r (1893 - 1918), N- ♪ -i- ♪ -vot- ♪ her li- to conducting and t- ♪ -hing. In 1937 she was th- ♪ -irst woman to conduct th- ♪ -oston Symphony Orchestra. She taught in Fran- ♪ -t th- ♪ -*ole Normal* ♪ -*Musique*, an- ♪ -meri- ♪ -n Conservatory in Fontain- ♪ -l- ♪ -u, and in the Unit- ♪ States at R- ♪ -li- ♪ -oll- ♪ -nd the Juilliard School. Among her many internationally known stu- ♪ -nts ar- ♪ -ron Coplan- ♪ -or- ♪ -rshwin, Th- ♪ Musgrav- ♪ -nd Walter Piston. For her ex- ♪ -ptional l- ♪ -y, N- ♪ -ia r- ♪ -iv- ♪ many awards including honorary doctorates from Oxfor- ♪ -nd Harvard.

FLORENCE BEATRICE PRICE (1888-1953)

Floren - [♪] - tri - [♪] Pri - [♪] ,

or - [♪] - nist, pianist, and t - [♪] - her, was the first

[♪] - ri - [♪] - n Ameri - [♪] - n woman to

[♪] - om - [♪] - mous for composing orchestral

works. She r - [♪] - iv - [♪] national [♪] - laim for her *Symphony No. 1*

in e minor, which the est - [♪] - m - [♪] Chi - [♪] - o Symphony Orchestra

premier - [♪] in 1933. Floren - [♪] is also lau - [♪] for her many art

songs, arran - [♪] - ments of spirituals, and piano pi - [♪] - s ([♪]

[♪] - n - [♪] - s in the [♪] - n - [♪] - rakes). [♪] - ter

[♪] - rly musi - [♪] - l encour - [♪] - ment from her mother, she studi - [♪]

or - [♪] - n, piano, and composition at the New Englan - [♪] - onservatory of Music in

Boston gr - uating with honors in 1906. Floren - taught music at th - otton Plant Ark - lphi - my and Shorter Coll - in Little Rock, Arkansas, then dir - t - the musi - partment of Clark Coll - in Atlanta. In 1912 she marri - and return - to Little Rock, her birthpl - . In 1927, the Pric - mily mov - to Chi - o where Florence - n to - ther - ol - s for her compositions. She play - the th - ter or - n for silent films, and wrote cham - r and or - n works. Most of her musi - l cr - tions, which interw - ve Romantic harmonies and her - ri - n Ameri - n cultural herit - , await publi - tion.

JEAN COULTHARD (1918-2000)

J - ♪ - n Coulthard was a prolifi - ♪

- n - ♪ - ian composer, pianist, and

pro - ♪ - ssor emeritus o - ♪ - omposition

from the University o - ♪ - ritish Columbia. She

studi - ♪ - music with her mother, a pianist who ♪ - vo - ♪ - t -

the music o - ♪ - ussy and Ravel, then with Ralph Vaughan Williams at the

Royal Coll - ♪ - of Music in London. Sh - ♪ - lso

r - ♪ - iv - ♪ - ncour - ♪ - ment from composers

- rius Milhau - ♪ , - ♪ - l - ♪ - rtok, and

N - ♪ - i - ♪ - oulan - ♪ - r. J - ♪ - n

compos - ♪ - orchestral (♪ - n - ♪ - ian

- ntasy (1939), cham - r (*Th* - irds of Landsdowne

(1972) with tap - irdsongs from Vancouver Island), piano (

p - ogi - l pi - s in th -

- n - ian Royal Conservatory of Music Series), and vo - l

musi - (*Thr* - *Shakesp* - re Sonnets (1947)). R - io

- n - International's *Anthology o* - n - ian

Music (1982) inclu - d her monologue *"Music is My Whole Li* - ." She

r - iv - many awards for her cr - tiv -

- orts includin - Royal Society - llowship for a year's study in

Fran - nd honorary doctorates by the University o - ritish

Columbi - n - oncordia University in Montreal.

PEGGY GLANVILLE-HICKS (1912-1990)

Image from http://www.pendragonpress.com/p_gh.html, accessed August 9, 2005; image modified by misumiwaDesign

P - [♪] - y Glanville - Hicks was an Australian composer, musi - [♪] - riti - [♪] - n - [♪] - vo - [♪] - te of new musi - [♪] - n - [♪] - omposers. A world traveler who int - [♪] - rat - [♪] - stern and Western i - [♪] - s, she studi - [♪] - t the Melbourn - [♪] - onservatorium, then with Ralph Vaughan Williams at the Royal Coll - [♪] - of Music in London, and Nadi - [♪] - oulan - [♪] - r in Paris. She liv - [♪] - in the Unit - [♪] - States from 1942 until 1959, then mov - [♪] - to Athens, Gr - [♪] - , and in 1976 return - [♪] - to Australia. She r - [♪] - iv - [♪] - ulbright [♪] - llowship (1961- 1963) to res - [♪] - rch [♪] - n musi - [♪] - n - [♪] - Rock - [♪] - ller grant (1961) to res - [♪] - rch in th - [♪] - r and Mi - [♪] - l - [♪]

- st. Pe - y compos - ham - r (

Sonat - *or Harp* (1951), orchestral (- trus - n Con - rto

(1956) for piano and orchestra), vo - l (*Thomsoniana* (1949) on words by Virgil

Thomson), opera (*Nausi* - (1961)), - llet, an - ilm music.

Sh - n - rlton Spr - ue Smith co-foun - the

International Musi - und to help r - st - lish Europ - n

artists - ter World War II. She was musi - riti - or the New York Herald

Tribune (1948-1958) an - ir - tor of the New York Composers' Forum (1950-1960).

In 1955, she help - Yehudi Menuhin or - niz - on - rts of

Indian musi - t the Museum of Mo - rn Art, where sh - lso

cr - t - on - rts of new Ameri - n music.

Marian McPartland (1918–2013)

Image from http://www.cnn.com/2004/SHOWBIZ/ Music/09/15/monterey.mcpartland/, accessed August 9, 2005; image modified by misumiwaDesign

Marian McPartland (Mar - ♪ - ret Marian Turner) was a l - ♪ - n - ♪ - ry British jazz pianist, improviser, composer, ♪ - u - ♪ - tor, and author. She was ♪ - mous for hosting *Marian McPartland's Piano Jazz* from 1978 until 2011 on National Public Radio in the Unit - ♪ States which r - ♪ - hed listeners in 25 countries. A musi - ♪ - l prodigy, she studi - ♪ - t th - ♪ - uildhall School of Music in London, then join - ♪ vau - ♪ - ville - t entertainin - ♪ - lli - ♪ troops in Europ - ♪ - uring World War II. While on tour in ♪ - lgium, she met an - ♪ - n to play with her future hus - ♪ - nd, Chi - ♪ - o cornetist Jimmy McPartland, with whom she mov - ♪ to Manhattan in 1949. Marian form - ♪ her own trio an - ♪ - n a long resi - ♪ - ncy (1952 - 1960) at th -   - m -   New York jazz club, Hickory House, a m -   - ting

pl -   - or jazz artists   - uke Ellington,   - nny Goodman, and

Os -   - r Peterson. She rel -   - s -   more than 50 albums with Concord

R -   - ords, e.g. *Music by Mary Lou Williams*, and foun -   her own l -   - l,

Halcyon R -   - ords. She also r -   - or -   her own compositions e.g. *Twilight*

World, In th -   *- ys of Our Love,* an -   - mbian -   nominat -

for a Grammy. In 1986 she was   - pt -   into the International Association of Jazz

- u -   - tion Hall of Fame. Her books inclu -   - *ll in Good Time*, jazz profiles

publish -   - y Oxford University Press in 1987. In her 1998   *Just Friends,* she

cel -   - rat -   her 80th birth -   - y playing duets with six other jazz artists including

- ve Bru -   - k and Geor -   Sh -   - ring.

ERZSEBÉT SZÖNYI (B.1924)

Erzs - ♪ - t Szönyi is a Hun - ♪ - rian t - ♪ - her, conductor, an - ♪ - omposer of vo - ♪ - l, piano, or - ♪ - n (♪ *Six Pi* - ♪ - s (1955)), cham - ♪ - r, st - ♪ -, and orchestral music. She gr - ♪ - uat - ♪ - from the Bu - ♪ - pest Liszt ♪ - my of Music, where she taught folk musi - ♪ - lasses for Zoltán Ko - ♪ - ly. Then she studi - ♪ - with Tony Aubin, N - ♪ - i - ♪ - oulan - ♪ - r, and Olivier Messi - ♪ - n in Paris where she r - ♪ - iv - ♪ - prize for her *Divertimento for Orchestra Nr. 1* (1948). From 1948 until 1981 she ♪ - vot - ♪

her li- to t- -hing music p- -ogy in the

Bu- -pest Liszt -my, where she worked with Ko- -ly.

She pro- to promote Kodaly's -u- -tional theories

-ro- as -oard mem- -r of the International

Society for Musi- -u- -tion. In 1960 Erzs- -t

-m- -irector of t- -her training at the Liszt

-my, and publish- her *Method of Musi-* -l

R- *-ing and Writing* (1953-65). In 2014 Jerry L. J- -ard published

-ook -out her lif- -ll- *Tear*

in the Curtain: The Musi- -l *Diplom-* -y *of Erzsébet Szönyi: Musician,*

Composer, T- -her *of T-* -hers.

SOFIA GUBAIDULINA (B. 1931)

Image from http://www.polarmusicprize.com/newSite/cerm2002_
photos.shtml, accessed August 9, 2005; image modified by
misumiwaDesign

Sofi - [music notation] - u - [music notation] - idulina

is an eminent Russian

avant - [music notation] - r - [music notation] -

[music notation] - omposer of orchestral,

vo - [music notation] - l ([music notation] *Alleluja*

(1990)), cham - [music notation] - r and solo instrumental music. Born in Tatarstan, she studi - [music notation]

piano at the Kazan' Stat - [music notation] - onservatory (1949-1954) an - [music notation] - omposition

at the Moscow Conservatory (1954-1963) with N. Peyko, and V. Sh - [music notation] - lin. In

1975 sh - [music notation] - st - [music notation] - lish - [music notation] - the improvisational group "Astreya"

with composers Artyomov and Suslin. Sofi - [music notation] - xplores sound, [music notation] with

percussion an - [music notation] - xotic instruments, spiritual r - [music notation] - onciliation of opposing for - s, (her or - n solo *Hell*

un - - unkel (1976), which is German for *Light an* - rk), and

new performing t - - hniques an - ombinations of instruments

(*In Cro* - (1979) for - llo and or - n).

Diverse influen - s on her cr - tive li -

inclu - ncient - yptian texts, the Fibonacci sequence, Omar

Khayyam, Hil - rd von Bin - n, the Bible, T.S. Eliot, and Rainer

Maria Rilke. Sofia has - ome internationally renown - in

Asi - , - urop - nd the Unit - States.

Sin - 1992 she has liv - in Hamburg, - rmany.

KIKUKO MASUMOTO (B. 1937)

増本 伎共子

Kikuko Masumoto is a Japanes - omposer

o - - ham - - r and vo - - l

music (Thr - songs from

m - - ieval Japan), and ethnomusicologist who wrote - ku:

Court Music in Japan (Tokyo, 1968). She sel - - ts ton - - olors

of tr - - itional Japanese instruments, shakuh - - hi

(an en - - lown flute) and koto (thirt - - n pluck - strings

with a long r - - tangular body and mov - - l -

- ri - - s), as well as Europ - - n instruments,

the piano for her pi- ♪ -s. ♪ -rly in her li- ♪ Kikuko

studi- ♪ piano with her mother, then ♪ -i- ♪ to

con- ♪ -ntrate on composition, harmony, counterpoint, and theory at the Toho

♪ -kuen School of Musi- ♪ , -n- ♪ ♪ -thnomusicology at

the University of Tokyo. In 1982 sh- ♪ ♪ -m- ♪ ♪ -ssistant

professor at Toho ♪ -kuen University. She is a mem- ♪ -r of the

Society for Res- ♪ -rch in Asiatic Musi- ♪ , ♪ -nd th- ♪

♪ - ontemporary Music Society of Japan.

ANOUSHKA SHANKAR (B. 1981)

Anoushka Shankar is ♪ - omposer, ex - ♪ - ptionally talent - ♪ sitar performer,

and half-sister of Norah Jones. She is continuing th - ♪

♪ - r - ♪ - t musi - ♪ - l

tr - ♪ - ition of Indi - ♪ - n - ♪

♪ - r - ♪ - tive l - ♪ - y of her ♪ - ther, th - ♪ - mous

sitar virtuoso an - ♪ - omposer Ravi Shankar. The sitar is a long n - ♪ - k - ♪ and

pluck - ♪ string instrument from India with mov - ♪ - l - ♪ - rets

an - ♪ roun - ♪ - our - ♪ - ody. Anoushka is the only artist to

♪ - ompletely train - ♪ - y her ♪ - ther, with whom she

perform - ♪ on st - ♪ - s around the worl - ♪. At the ♪ of

Image from http://www.floridatheatre.com/events_detail.
asp?EventID=630, accessed July 10, 2005; image modified by
misumiwaDesign

56

thirt - [♩] - n sh - [♩] - [♩] - ut -: [♩] as a sitarist in New [♩] - lhi, India,

th - [♩] - [♩] - ity where the Ravi Shankar [♩] - ntre is lo - [♩] - t - [♩]. She

has rel - [♩] - s - [♩] the following [♩]s: *Anoushka* (1998), *Anourag* (2000), *Anoushka*

Shankar Liv - [♩] - t [♩] - *rnegie Hall* (2001), *Ris* - [♩] (2005), *Traveller* (2011), and

Home (2015). Born and rais - [♩] in London by her mother Sukanya, when Anoushka

was [♩] - leven, th - [♩] - mily mov - [♩] to Encinitas,

- liforni - [♩]. Anoushka has [♩] - n internationally honor - [♩] - or her

extraordinary artistry and musicianship. She is the youn - [♩] - st an - [♩] - irst

- male to r - [♩] - ive th - [♩] - ritish Parliament House

o - [♩] - ommons Shield (1998). Anoushka's [♩] - r - [♩] - r is blossoming.

TIME PERIOD AND NATIONALITY QUIZ

Solve the following puzzle which matches each composer to her country of birth and the era in which she lived/lives. If you are unsure of the solution, read through the biographies again. Each includes a clue to the origin of the composer.

— Ancient Sumeri - 🎼 : 🎼 - nh - 🎼 - uanna

— M - 🎼 - ieval Gr - 🎼 - k: Kassi - 🎼

— 🎼 - rman: Hil - 🎼 - rd von Bin - 🎼 - n

— Renaissan - 🎼 Italian: M - 🎼 - len - 🎼 - sulana

— 🎼 - roqu - 🎼 - rench: Eliz - 🎼 - th J - 🎼 - quet

🎼 - l - 🎼 - uerre

— Italian: Fran - 🎼 - s - 🎼 - ini

— Classi - 🎼 - l Austrian: Maria Theresia von Par - 🎼 - is

— 🎼 - rman: Ann - 🎼 - malia

— Romantic Polish: Mari - 🎼 - ta Szymanowsk - 🎼

— 🎼 - rman: Clara Wi - 🎼 - k Schumann

— Venezuelan: Teres - 🎼 - rreño

— Brazilian: Chiquinh - 🎼 - onz - 🎼

— Hawaiian: Qu - 🎼 - n Lili'oukalani

— Norw - 𝄢 - ian: 🎼 - th - 𝄢 🎼 - ker - Grøn - 🎼 - hl

— English: 🎼 - m - 🎼 🎼 - thel Smyth

— Ameri - 𝄢 - n: Amy 🎼 - h

— 20th - 🎼 - ntury 𝄢 - ri - 𝄢 - n - Ameri - 𝄢 - n:

Floren - 𝄢 - Pri - 🎼

— French: N - 🎼 - i - 𝄢 🎼 - oulan - 🎼 - r

— Australian: P - 🎼 - y Glanville - Hicks

— 🎼 - n - 𝄢 - ian: J - 🎼 - n Coulthard

— 21st 𝄢 - ntury Russian: Sofi - 🎼 🎼 - u - 𝄢 - idulina

— Hun - 🎼 - rian: Erzs - 🎼 - t Szönyi

— English: M - 🎼 - rian McPartland

— Jap - 𝄢 - nese: Kikuko Masumoto

— Indian: 🎼 - noushka Shankar

WORLD MAP

This world map shows the birth countries of the composers included in this book.

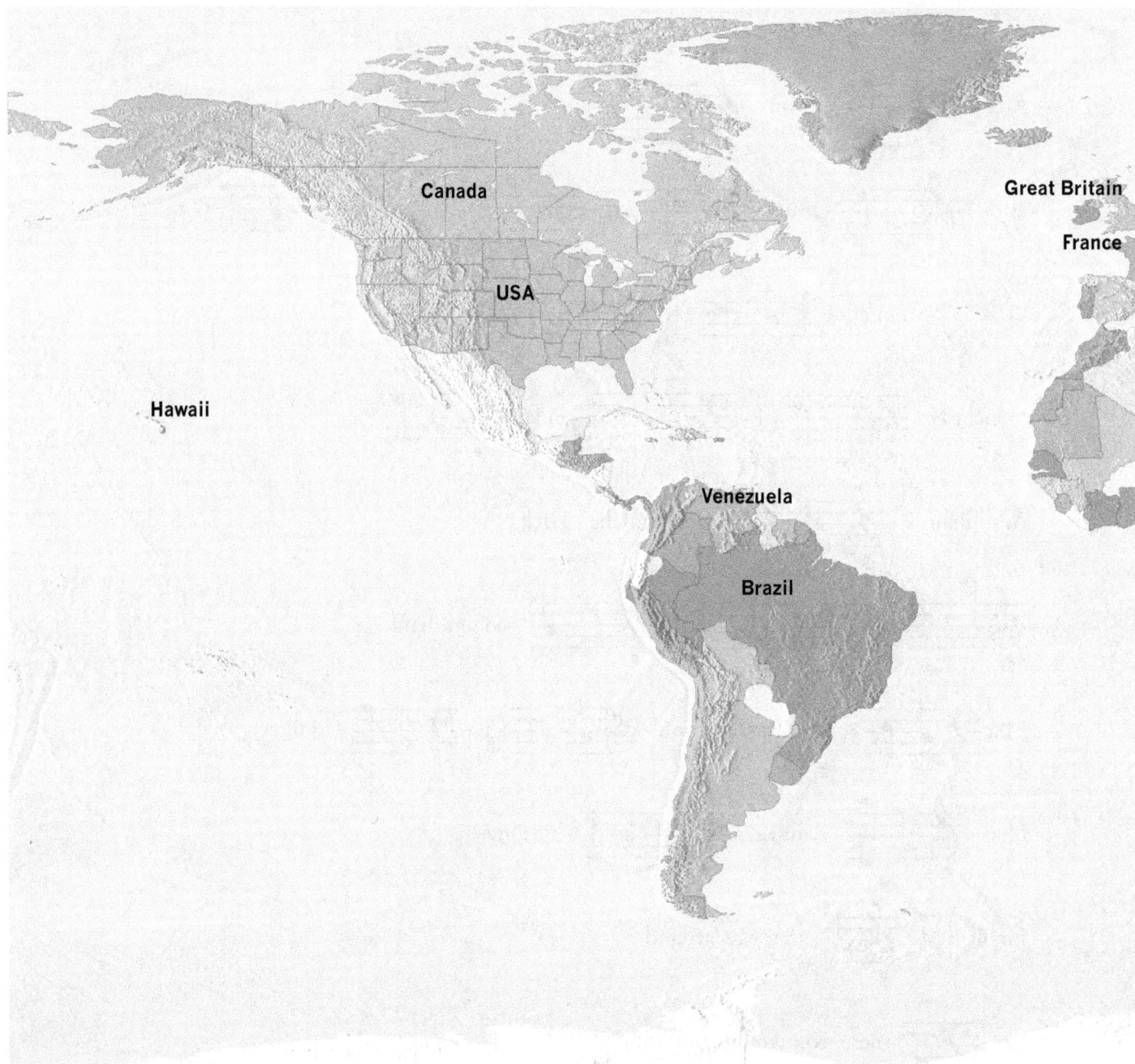

Canada

Great Britain

France

USA

Hawaii

Venezuela

Brazil

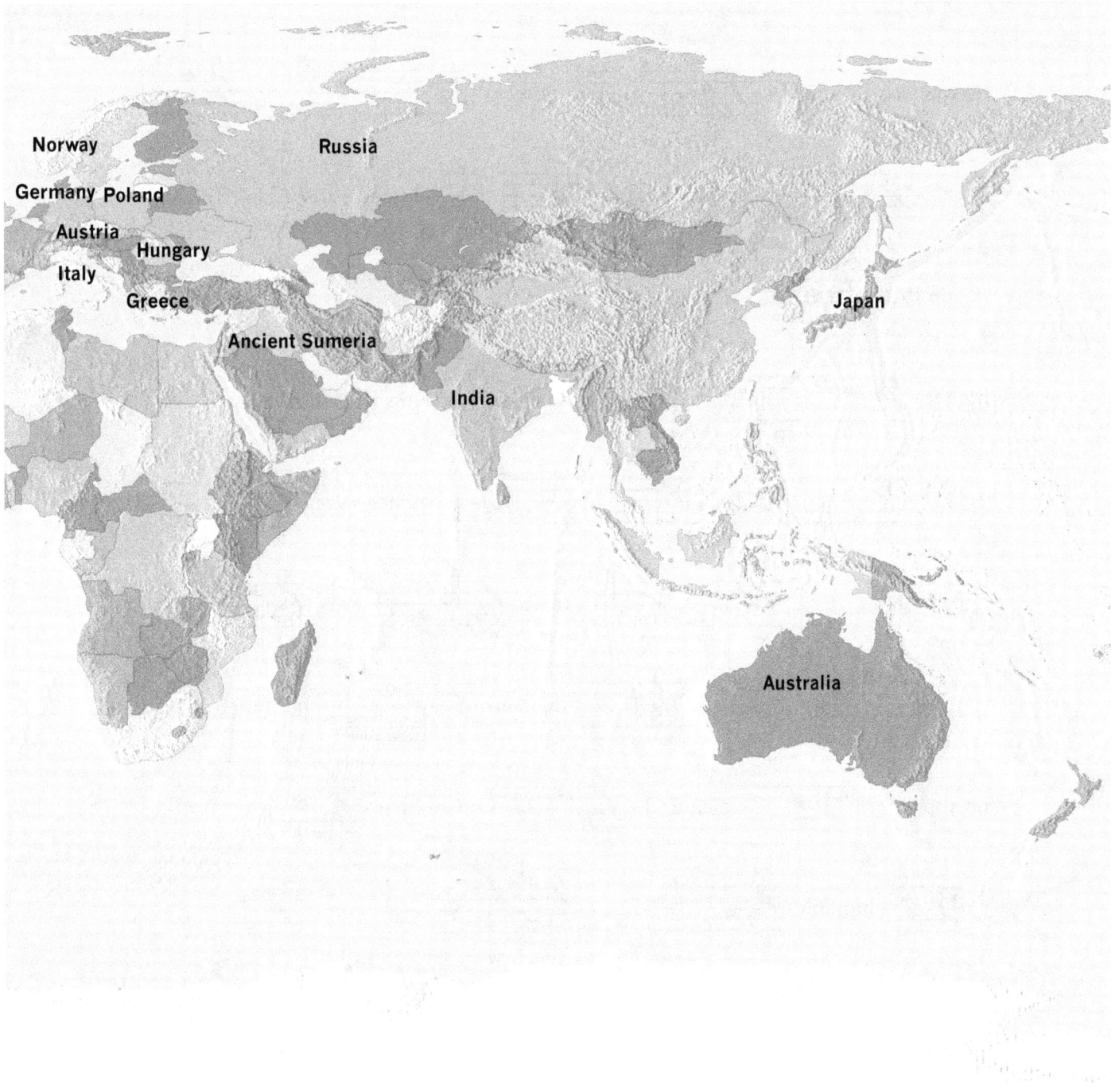

Norway

Germany Poland

Austria

Hungary

Italy

Greece

Ancient Sumeria

Russia

Japan

India

Australia

Quiz Questions

1. Who was h - 𝄢 - ring impair - 𝄞 - ?
   𝄞 - th - 𝄢 - ker-Grøn - 𝄞 - hl,
   𝄞 - m - 𝄞 - thel Smyth.

2. Who was visually impair - 𝄢 - nd help - 𝄢 - r - 𝄞 - te
   th - 𝄢 - irst school for th - 𝄢 - lind in Paris? Maria Theresia
   von Par - 𝄢 - is.

3. Who wer - 𝄢 - on - 𝄞 - rt pianists? Maria Theresia von
   Par - 𝄢 - is, Mari - 𝄞 - ta Szymanowsk - 𝄞 - , lara
   Schumann, Teres - 𝄞 - rreño, 𝄞 - th - 𝄞
   𝄞 - ker-Grøn - 𝄞 - hl, Amy 𝄞 - h, Marian McPartland.

4. Who also studi - 𝄢 - piano? J - 𝄞 - n Coulthar - 𝄞 - ,
   𝄢 - hiquinh - 𝄞 - onz - 𝄞 - , nn - 𝄢
   𝄢 - mali - 𝄞 - , loren - 𝄞 - Pri - 𝄞 - , Sofi - 𝄞

- u - - idulina, Qu - - n Lili'oukalani, Kikuko Masumoto,

Anoushka Shankar ;-)

5. Who is a virtuoso sitarist? Anoushka Shankar ;-)

6. Who were sin - - rs?

M - - len - - sulan - ,

- ran - - s - - ini,

Teres - - rreño.

7. Who - m - - rom musi - - l - milies?

Eliz - - th J - - quet l - - uerre,

Ann - - mali - , lara Schumann,

Teres - - rreño, Amy - h,

N - - i - - oulan - - r, J - - n Coulthard.

8. Who were nuns? Kassia, Hil - - rd von Bin - - n.

9. Who wer - [note] - omposers in courts? Enh - [note] - uann - [note], - [note] - ran - [note] - s - [note] [note] - ini, Eliz - [note] - th - [note] - l - [note] - uerr - [note], - nn - [note] - malia, Mari - [note] [note] - ta Szymanowska, Qu - [note] - n Lili'oukalani.

10. Who are university/conservatory pro - [note] - ssors of music? Clara Schumann, N - [note] - i - [note] - oulan - [note] - r, Marian McPartlan - [note], - rzs - [note] - t Szönyi, Floren - [note] Pri - [note], J - [note] - n Coulthard, Kikuko Masumoto.

11. Who was th - [note] - irst woman to conduct an orchestra in Brazil? Chiquinh - [note] - onz - [note].

12. Who was th - [note] - irst woman to conduct th - [note] - oston Symphony Orchestra? N - [note] - i - [note] - oulan - [note] - r.

13. Who est - [note] - lish - [note] - famous library? Ann - [note] - malia.

64

14. Who host - [musical notation] National Public R - [musical notation] - io jazz program for more than

twenty-five y - [musical notation] - rs? Marian McPartland ;-)

15. Who is an author o - [musical notation] - ooks, poetry, critiques...? Enh - [musical notation] - uanna,

Kassia, Hil - [musical notation] - rd von Bin - [musical notation] - n, Qu - [musical notation] - n

Lili'oukalani, [musical notation] - m - [musical notation] - thel Smyth, P - [musical notation] - y

Glanville-Hicks, Kikuko Masumoto, Erzs - [musical notation] - t Szönyi, Marian McPartland.

16. Who is th - [musical notation] - rliest known woman composer an - [musical notation] - uthor?

Enh - [musical notation] - uanna.

17. Who wrote m - [musical notation] - i - [musical notation] - l tr - [musical notation] - tises

an - [musical notation] - hants? Hil - [musical notation] - rd von Bin - [musical notation] - n.

18. Who was a musi - [musical notation] - riti - [musical notation] - or the New York Herald Tribune?

P - [musical notation] - y Glanville-Hicks.

19. Who interw - [musical notation] - ves [musical notation] - stern and Western music? Qu - [musical notation] - n

Lili'oukalani, Teres - [♪] - rreño, P - [♪] - y Glanville-Hicks,

Sofi - [♪] - u - [♪] - idulina, Kikuko Masumoto, Floren - [♪]

Pri - [♪] .

20. Who compos - [♪] vo - [♪] - l music? Enh - [♪] - uanna, Kassia,

Hil - [♪] - rd von Bin - [♪] - n, M - [♪] - len -

[♪] - sulan - [♪] , - ran - [♪] - s - [♪] - ini,

Eliz - [♪] - th J - [♪] - quet [♪] l - [♪] - uerre,

Maria Theresia von Par - [♪] - is, Mari - [♪] - ta Szymanowska,

Qu - [♪] - n Lili'oukalani, Chiquinh - [♪] - onz - [♪] ,

[♪] - m - [♪] - thel Smyth, Amy [♪] - h,

[♪] - the [♪] - ker-Grøn - [♪] - hl,

N - [♪] - i - [♪] - oulan - [♪] - r, J - [♪] - n

Coulthard, P - [♪] - y Glanville-Hicks,

Sofi - [♪] - u - [♪] - idulina, Kikuko Masumoto.

21. Who compos - [music notation] - ham - [music notation] - r music? Eliz - [music notation] - th

J - [music notation] - quet [music notation] l - [music notation] - uerre,

Chiquinh - [music notation] - onz - [music notation], [music notation] - m - [music notation] - thel

Smyth, Amy Marcy Cheney [music notation] - h, J - [music notation] - n Coulthard,

P - [music notation] - y Glanville-Hicks, Erzs - [music notation] - t Szönyi,

Sofi - [music notation] - u - [music notation] - idulina, Kikuko Masumoto.

22. Who compos - [music notation] harpsichord pi - [music notation] - s? Eliz - [music notation] - th

J - [music notation] - quet [music notation] l - [music notation] - uerre.

23. Who wrote piano compositions? Maria Theresia von Par - [music notation] - is,

Mari - [music notation] - ta Szymanowska, Clara Schumann,

Teres - [music notation] - rreño, [music notation] - the [music notation] - ker-

Grøn - [music notation] - hl, Erzs - [music notation] - t Szönyi, Floren - [music notation]

Pri - [music notation], Marian McPartland, Sofi - [music notation] - u - [music notation] - idulina.

24. Who compos- [♪] organ works? Eliz- [♪] -th J- [♪] -quet

[♪] -l- [♪] [♪] -uerre, Clara Schumann, Erzs- [♪] -t Szönyi,

Florence Pri- [♪], Sofi- [♪] [♪] -u- [♪] -idulina, Amy

[♪] -h, N- [♪] -i- [♪] -oulan- [♪] -r.

25. Who compos- [♪] orchestral works? Chiquinh- [♪] [♪] -onz- [♪],

Floren- [♪] Pri- [♪], Dam- [♪] [♪] -thel Smyth, Amy

[♪] -h, J- [♪] -n Coulthard, P- [♪] -y Glanville-

Hicks, Erzs- [♪] -t Szönyi, Sofi- [♪] [♪] -u- [♪] -idulina.

26. Who is th- [♪] [♪] -irst known [♪] -ri- [♪] -n-

Ameri- [♪] -n [♪] -mal- [♪] [♪] -omposer of orchestral works?

Floren- [♪] Pri- [♪].

27. Who is th- [♪] [♪] -irst woman known to compose m- [♪] -ri- [♪] -ls?

M- [♪] -len- [♪] [♪] -sulana.

28. Who is th - 🎵 - irst woman known to compose operas?

Fran - 🎵 - s - 🎵 - ini.

29. Who compos - 🎵 - harpsichord pi - 🎵 - s and

pion - 🎵 - r - 🎵 - 🎵 - rench 🎵 - ntatas?

Eliz - 🎵 - th 🎵 - l - 🎵 - uerre.

30. Who were social 🎵 - tivists? 🎵 - m - 🎵 - thel Smyth,

Chiquinh - 🎵 - 🎵 - onz - 🎵 - .

Face and Name Quiz

Write the matching name of each women composer under her image. If you are not sure, go back to the biographies to check your answer.

1.

2.

3.

4.

5.

6.

7.

8.

9.

10.

11.

12.

13.

14.

15.

16.

17.

18.

19.

20.

21.

22.

23.

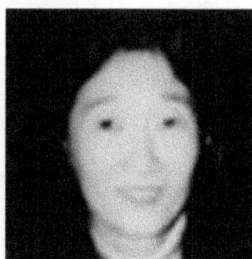
24.

25.

Answers:

1. Amy Marcy Cheney Beach; 2. Anna Amalia; 3. Anoushka Shankar; 4. Agathe Backer-Grøndahl; 5. Nadia Boulanger; 6. Teresa Carreño; 7. Clara Wieck Schumann; 8. Jean Coulthard; 9. Enheduanna; 10. Erzsébet Szőnyi; 11. Dame Ethel Smyth; 12. Florence Price; 13. Francesca Caccini; 14. Peggy Glanville-Hicks; 15. Chiquinha Gonzaga; 16. Sofia Gubaidulina; 17. Hildegard von Bingen; 18. Elizabeth Jacquet de la Guerre; 19. Kassia; 20. Queen Lili'uokalani; 21. Maddalena Casulana; 22. Marian McPartland; 23. Maria Agata Szymanowska; 24. Kikuko Masumoto; 25. Maria Theresia von Paradis

70

Battersby, Christine. *Gender and Genius: Towards a Feminist Aesthetic.* Bloomington and Indianapolis: Indiana University Press, 1989.

Block, Adrienne Fried. *Women in American Music: A Bibliography of Music and Literature.* Westport, CT: Greenwood Press, 1988.

Borroff, Edith. *An Introduction to Elisabeth-Claude Jacquet de la Guerre.* Brooklyn, NY: Institute of Mediaeval Music, Ltd., 1683 West 8th Street, 1966.

Bowers, Jane and Judith Tick, eds. *Women Making Music: The Western Art Tradition 1150-1950.* Urbana and Chicago: University of Illinois Press, 1986.

Bowers, Jane M. "Feminist Scholarship and the Field of Musicology: I and II" *College Music Symposium*, Vol. 29 (1989) 81-99, and Vol. 30 (Spring 1990) 1-13.

Briscoe, James R., ed. *Historical Anthology of Music by Women.* Bloomington, Indiana: Indiana University Press, 1987. (recordings available)

Briscoe, James R., ed. *Contemporary Anthology of Music by Women.* Bloomington: Indiana University Press, 1997.

Broude Brothers Ltd., 141 White Oaks Rd., Williamstown, MA 01267 (Choral Packet: Music by Women Composers)

California State University Northridge, Oviatt Library, Northridge, CA 91330 (Aaron Cohen Collection)

Citron, Marcia J. *Gender and the Musical Canon.* New York: Cambridge University Press, 1993.

ClarNan Editions, Barbara Garvey Jackson, 235 Baxter Lane, Fayetteville, Arkansas 72701 (Early Music by Women Composers)

Cohen, Aaron I. *International Encyclopedia of Women Composers.* (2 volumes) New York: NY 10025: Books and Music, P.O. Box 1301, Cathedral Station, 1987.

College Music Society. *Report Number 5: Women's Studies/ Women's Status.* Boulder, CO: The College Music Society, Inc., 1988.

Cook, Susan C. "Women, Women's Studies, Music and Musicology: Issues of Pedagogy and Scholarship," *College Music Symposium*, Vol. 29 (1989) 81-99.

Cook, Susan C. and Judy S. Tsou, eds. *Cecilia Reclaimed: Feminist Perspectives on Gender and Music*. Urbana: University of Illinois Press, 1993.

Degenhardt, Gertrude. *Musikfrauen-Women in Music*. Koblenz, Germany: Mittelrhein-Museum.

Edition Donna, Hardtstrasse 25, Düsseldorf, Germany.

Ehrenreich, Barbara and Deirdre English. *For Her Own Good: 150 Years of the Experts' Advice to Women*. Garden City, NY: Anchor Books, 1978.

Furore Edition, Naumburger Str. 40, D-34127 Kassel, Germany, www.furore-verlag.de

Glickman, Sylvia & Martha Furman Schleifer. *Women Composers: Music Through the Ages*. New York: G.K. Hall & Co., 1998.

Hayles, N. Katherine. *Chaos Bound: Orderly Disorder in Contemporary Literature and Science*. Ithaca, NY: Cornell University, 1990.

Heinrich, Adel. *Organ and Harpsichord Music by Women Composers*. Westport, CT: Greenwood Press, 1991.

Hildegard Publishing Company, Box 332, Bryn Mawr, PA 19010, www.hildegard.com

Hoffmann, Freia. *Instrument und Körper*. Frankfurt am Main: Insel Verlag, Taschenbuch 1274, 1991.

International Alliance for Women in Music; www.iawm.org

International Women Composers Library, Dr. Miriam Zach, Director; www.iwclib.org

Jezic, Diane Peacock. *Women Composers: The Lost Tradition Found*. New York: The Feminist Press at the City University of New York, 1988.

Koskoff, Ellen, ed. *Women and Music in Cross-Cultural Perspective*. Westport, CT: Greenwood Press, 1987.

Ladyslipper Inc., P.O. Box 3124-R, Durham, NC 27715; orders@ladyslipper.org

LePage, Jane Weiner. *Women Composers, Conductors, and Musicians of the Twentieth Century.* Metuchen, NJ: The Scarecrow Press, Inc., 1980.

Macy, Laura W., "Women's history and early music" in *Companion to Medieval and Renaissance Music*, Tess Knighton and David Fallows, eds. New York: Schirmer Books, 1992.

Marshall, Kimberly, ed. *Rediscovering the Muses: Women's Musical Traditions.* Boston: Northeastern University Press, 1993.

McClary, Susan. *Feminine Endings: Music, Gender, and Sexuality.* Minnesota: University of Minnesota Press, 1991.

Murphy, Cullen. "Women and the Bible" in *The Atlantic Monthly* (August 1993) 39-45, 48, 50-55, 58, 60, 62, 64.

Neuls-Bates, Carol. *Women in Music: An Anthology of Source Readings from the Middle Ages to the Present.* New York: Harper-Row, 1982.

Offen, Karen, Ruth Roach Pierson and Jane Rendall, eds. *Writing Women's History: International Perspectives.* Bloomington and Indianapolis: Indiana University Press, 1991.

Olivier, Antje and Karin Weingartz-Perschel. *Komponistinnen von A-Z.* Düsseldorf: Tokkata Verlag für Frauenforschung, 1988.

Olivier, Antje & Sevgi Braun, eds. *Komponistinnen aus 800. Jahren.* Essen, Germany: Sequentia-Verlag, 1996.

Pendle, Karin, ed. *Women and Music, A History.* Bloomington: Indiana University Press, 2001.

Rieger, Eva. *Frau, Musik & Männerherrschaft.* Kassel: Furore-Verlag, Edition 828, 1988.

Rieger, Eva, ed. *Frau und Musik.* Kassel: Furore-Verlag, Edition 844, 1990.

Sadie, Julie Anne & Rhian Samuel, eds. *The New Grove Dictionary of Women Composers.* London: Macmillan Press Ltd, 1995.

Solie, Ruth A., ed. *Musicology and Difference: Gender and Sexuality in Music Scholarship.* Berkeley: University of California Press, 1993.

Spretnak, Charlene, ed. *The Politics of Women's Spirituality: Essays on the Rise of Spiritual Power within the Feminist Movement.* Garden City, NY: Anchor Books, 1982.

Stolba, K. Marie. *The Development of Western Music: A History.* 2nd edition. Dubuque, IA: Brown & Benchmark, 1994.

Sweet Honey in the Rock, Flying Fish Records, 1304 W. Schubert, Chicago, IL 60614.

Vivace Press, University of Missouri-St. Louis, One University Boulevard, 265 Arts Administration Building, St. Louis, MO 63121 (scores & *Women of Note Quarterly*); vivacepress@umsl.edu.

Walker-Hill, Helen, ed. *Black Women Composers: A Century of Piano Music (1893-1990).* Bryn Mawr, PA: Hildegard Publishing Company.

Zach, Miriam. *Hidden Treasures: 300 Years of Organ Music by Women Composers.* Recorded in Princeton University Chapel, Minerva Productions, 1998. (Available from www.iwclib.org)

Zaimont, Judith L., editor-in-chief. *The Musical Woman: An International Perspective* (2 vols.) Westport, CT: Greenwood Press, 1987.